let us play I SPY camping!

D1418276

i spy play books by
© Little Starry Dezign

ready to play
i spy camping?

just like real i spy game, letters
are not in alphabetical order.

spy with my little
eye, something beginning with...

spy with my little
eye, something beginning with...

C is for... campfire!

spy with my little
eye, something beginning with...

l is for...

lantern!

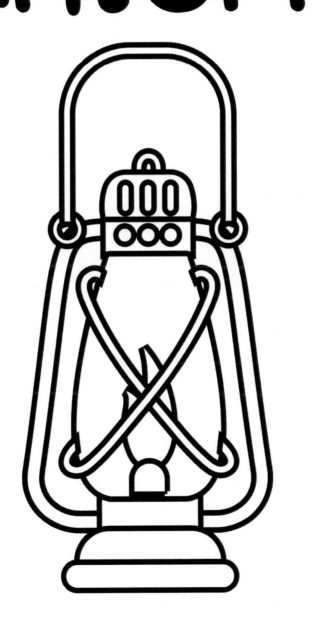

spy with my little
eye, something beginning with...

M is for... mushrooms!

spy with my little
eye, something beginning with...

C is for...
camera!

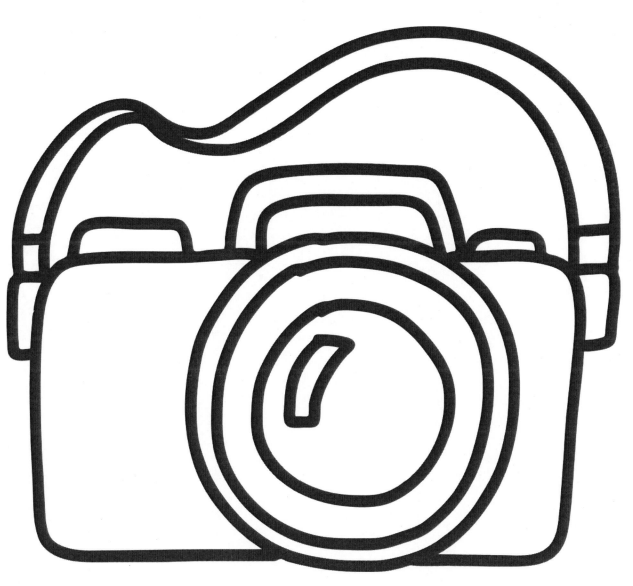

spy with my little
eye, something beginning with...

b is for... bear!

spy with my little

eye, something beginning with...

a is for...

axe!

spy with my little
eye, something beginning with...

t is for...

tent!

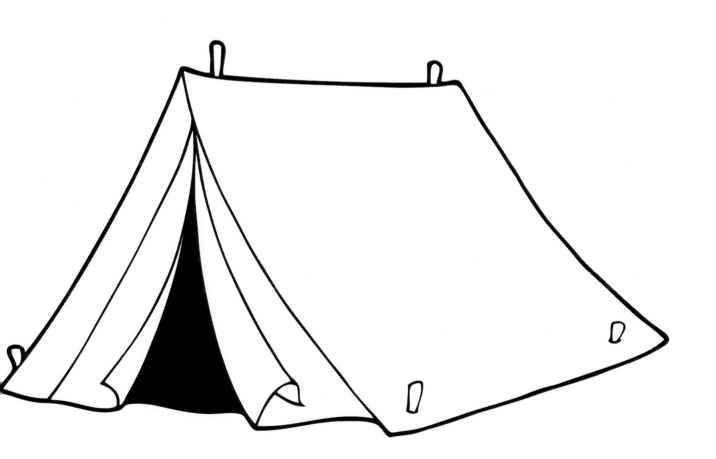

spy with my little
eye, something beginning with...

S is for...
squirrel!

spy with my little
eye, something beginning with...

K is for...
kite!

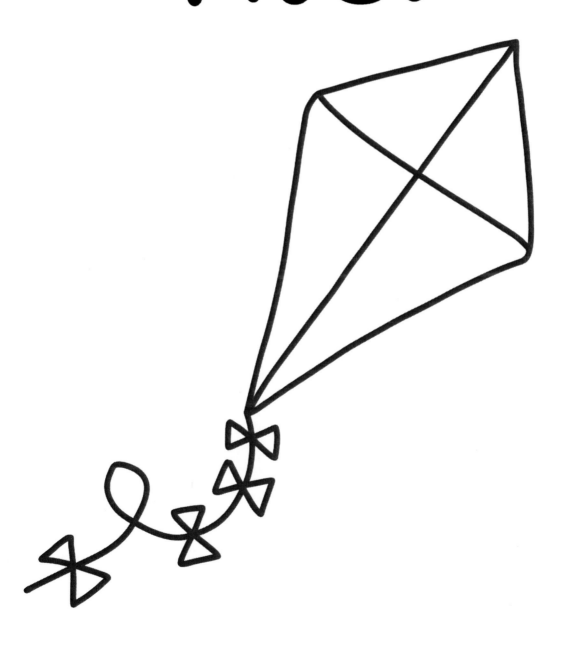

spy with my little
eye, something beginning with...

g is for...

guitar!

spy with my little eye, something beginning with...

M is for... map!

spy with my little eye, something beginning with...

h is for...

hat!

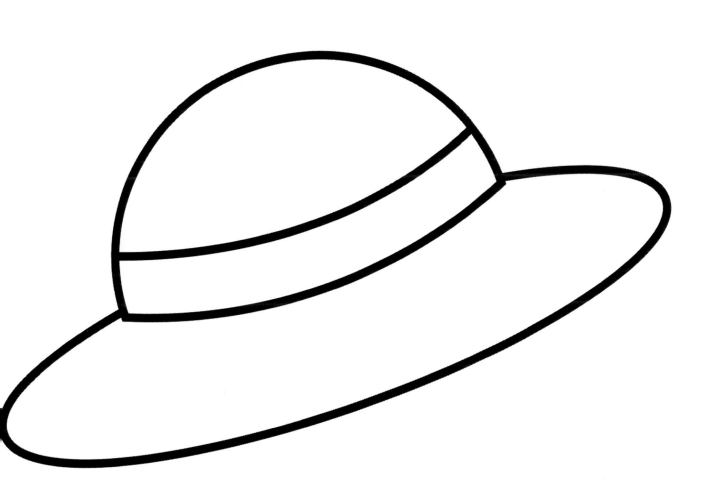

spy with my little
eye, something beginning with...

f is for...

flower!

spy with my little
eye, something beginning with...

W is for...
water bottle!

spy with my little
eye, something beginning with...

U is for...
umbrella!

spy with my little
eye, something beginning with...

S is for...
shovel!

spy with my little eye, something beginning with...

r is for...

rope!

spy with my little
eye, something beginning with...

b is for...
backpack!

Made in United States
North Haven, CT
21 October 2021